The Kids' Guide to Getting Your Words on Paper

. . . .

Simple Stuff to Build the Motor Skills and Strength for Handwriting

Lauren Brukner

Illustrated by Elissa Elwick

Jessica Kingsley Publishers
London and Philadelphia

The fonts, layout and overall design of this book have been prepared according to dyslexia friendly principles. At JKP we aim to make our books' content accessible to as many readers as possible.

First published in 2020
by Jessica Kingsley Publishers
73 Collier Street
London N1 9BE, UK
and
400 Market Street, Suite 400
Philadelphia, PA 19106, USA

www.jkp.com

Library of Congress Cataloging in Publication Data
A CIP catalog record for this book is available from the Library of Congress

British Library Cataloguing in Publication Data
A CIP catalogue record for this book is available from the British Library

ISBN 978 1 78775 156 9
eISBN 978 1 78775 157 6

Printed and bound in Great Britain

 Downloadable symbol

CONTENTS

How This Book Works and What You Will Find in It— A Note for Grown-Ups

(and Any Kids Who Like to Know This Kind of Boring Stuff)

Each of the five chapters in this book covers a different area. There's a note about the tripod pencil grasp and pencil grips... And a quiz which your child can take to see which chapter might be most relevant to them, to start with, or you can just use every chapter in the order I've written them.

You don't need to work through the chapters in a particular order, and you can, and should if possible, repeat chapters, and strategies, going back to them to see how your child is progressing.

Each of the main chapters contains the following:

Hand warm-up exercise summary instructions

These hand warm-ups are super important for all aspects of writing. They are so important that we introduce them with full instructions, before we go into the five main chapters, and we have also included a Hand Warm-Up star chart on page 22 which you can also download from https://libraryjkp.papertrell.com/redeem using the code VYOWUWA if you need spare copies.

Then we repeat the short exercise sequence at the start of each chapter. This is to encourage your child to do them several times a day.

There are also handy bookmark reminders that you can print off from Appendix 2 at the end of the book, for children to take to school or stick on the wall by their desk.

Kit lists
At the start of each of the five chapters you'll find a summary list of the kit you will need for the activities in the chapter, which is also a kind of contents list for the chapter. These are accompanied by some of Elissa's amazing drawings.

Longer explanations of the strategies for each chapter
These are illustrated fully, with step-by-step instructions and a rationale showing how they help. These are a mixture of activities and tools, most of which are either available as downloads in this book, or are everyday items you should have in the home or are found in the child's school.

"Let's get writing!" lines
These are lines where your child can practice writing a phrase or word, to see the effect of the strategy they just tried. They don't have to write after every activity—this is just there for them if they wish to write. You could write after some activities one day, then others on subsequent occasions. Sometimes your child might just want to doodle on the lines. That's fine too. There are two different sizes of line spacing provided; your child can choose the one that suits them that day.

"How did that go?" with emojis
This is an activity for your child to complete, after they've worked through the strategies in the chapter. They should circle how the activity made them feel. Then they should enter the ones they gave

a smiley face to into their Track My Progress chart. At first you can support them with this, but encourage them to develop the skills to assess their own progress if you can, so that they begin to complete these sheets on their own at the end of each session or chapter.

Track My Progress sheets

These are charts to help your child keep track of the strategies they used from each chapter, including how often they use them, and how helpful they find them.

Remember that the more often a child uses each chosen strategy, making sure they do it the same each time, the more helpful it will be.

Discourage your child from saying "this won't work" about a strategy. Suggest gently that they try it first. And give it a fair chance (that means more than once).

You can then use the Tracking my Progress charts together to see how things are changing for your child over time.

The appendices

This section contains the additional materials you will need for some of the strategies, carefully cross referenced to the relevant chapters, such as hand–eye coordination activities, bookmarks, and different types of paper for your child to try out, as well as useful At-a-Glance menus of the strategies from the chapters, to encourage your child to take control of their own routines for supporting their writing. Everything in the appendices is downloadable from https://libraryjkp. papertrell.com/redeem using the code VYOWUWA, and there are additional resources on there as well, such as colored paper and Handwriting Workbook worksheets for all the letters of the alphabet.

PART 1
FOR KIDS

Hey Kids, Let Me Tell You a Little About Me and This Book!

Hi, I'm Sketch!

Do you find writing tricky sometimes? Do other people sometimes find it hard to read what you've written?

Then you're in the right place!

Writing is one of those subjects that I am usually called in to help out with as I am an occupational therapist for kids.

So, what's an occupational therapist? We are not doctors (don't worry, no shots!). We don't give medicine, although I do think our work with kids can be just as helpful! Occupational therapists, no matter who we work with, provide tools, tips, and strategies to help our clients (the kids we work with!) be as independent and confident as possible.

That means, to empower you to do stuff on your own.

I absolutely love that. How great do you feel when you can, for example, do an art project all by yourself? What about ride a bike? Do a challenging numbers problem?

Can you think of a time when you had trouble with an activity and needed support from a grown-up? Maybe it was a parent, a grandparent, a teacher, or a therapist. Was there a point where you had an "Ah ha!" moment and you were able to do that activity on your own?

Those are my favorite moments as an occupational therapist. Those are our goals—helping you to achieve.

What is extra fun is that sometimes the path to get to that do-it-on-your-own moment may look a bit different for you than it does for other kids, say in a particular area, like writing and handwriting—and that is totally ok! Everybody needs their own support, and has their own journey.

Ok, now that you (I hope!) understand what occupational therapists do in general, let's see what the connection is to this book, shall we?

I support students in a bunch of different ways in the classroom or at home when they have trouble with writing—not with the actual coming-up-with-ideas part, necessarily (remember, I am definitely not a teacher!), but with the behind-the-scenes, get-your-hands-brain-and-body-ready stuff.

★ Is your body ready to write?

★ Are you sitting the right way?

★ How is your pencil grip?

★ Do you form the letters easily?

★ How about the lines on the paper? Are they easy to see?

★ Does your brain feel connected to your body?

Those are some of my areas. And the motivation behind why I decided to write this book!

I love creating guides for kids, where you can learn about all the different strategies, tools, and supports that will help you with different activities that may feel challenging—in this case, writing! I know that writing can make you feel *frustrated*, *wiggly*, or *tired*. It can sometimes even make your hand ache.

The fun activities and tools in this handwriting book will support you to write more and feel more confident—and comfortable—when you are writing.

HOW TO USE THIS BOOK

Remember, this is your book. You can read it cover to cover, or you can pick the chapters that sound most helpful to you! (You can even write in this book... There's a quiz coming up to help you find out more about yourself and what areas you might want to work on first, too.)

 Do you have trouble sitting up straight or keeping still when you're writing? Then go to Chapter 1 about Big Body Stuff to get some ideas.

 Is it hard for you to keep your eyes in the right place on the page during writing? Try out Chapter 2 on Helping Your Eyes Out.

 Do your hands ache when you write, and does writing make you tired way before it makes your friends tired? Can your friends get more writing done than you, in the same time? Then go to Chapter 3 about When Your Hands Just Feel Tired.

Does sitting at your table and concentrating on your writing make you feel super wriggly and distracted? Try Chapter 4 with its strategies for When it's Hard to Focus.

Do you feel as if you are always fiddling with stuff on your desk or maybe hanging upside down? Try out Chapter 5 on When All Your Body's Feelings and Senses Get Too Much (or Too Little).

It's up to you to decide how you are feeling! This is one of the skills this book will help you with.

You can choose your just-right strategies. Think of the chapters in this book as a menu! You might feel different and so pick different strategies to try out on different days to support you to do your best writing.

Before the chapters begin, you will find a quiz that is designed to help you figure out your own unique difficulties that may be impacting your writing.

Once you pinpoint your area or areas of difficulty, go to that chapter in this guide. Choose one or a few strategies to help you as you write.

Remember, this book is for you.

You can use it however you like. One day you might want to try the ideas in one chapter, another day, you can look at a different part of the book.

A Note About the Tripod Pencil Grip

Have you been given a pencil grip to use in school? Sometimes teachers will give kids grips to support their writing. They might tell you you're not holding your pencil the right way. This can be kind of embarrassing if your friends don't have to use a grip. But it's cool too because there are so many different kinds of grip to choose from—and they come in a lot of different colors you can collect.

And guess what? I have to tell you, I don't hold the pencil "the right way" either! My middle finger presses pretty hard, and my index finger does a kind of wrap-around-underneath-the-thumb kind of deal.

But guess what? I have pretty neat handwriting, even though it's not that standard "three finger in a perfect tripod" deal.

Lots of kids I see have their own grasp on the pencil as unique as their personality. As long as they can write and draw in a way that is functional, amazing!

So I wouldn't get too hung up about your "tripod grasp."

But at the same time, holding your pencil in what one might

call a weak or wacky grip *can* be a sign things aren't going so well with your writing.

When your grasp is not in a tripod (where the pointing and ring fingers cross to meet the thumb) and your writing and drawing or coloring is not functional—maybe people can't read it, or it makes you feel uncomfortable to hold a pencil too long—that's where I would say that your grasp may require some support from a grip. The pencil grip can support you to develop a stronger tripod grasp pattern.

Chapter 3 has a section that talks more about grips. There are many types of pencil grips to support the way you physically hold a pencil; check out that chapter for more information. (There are also some special pencil grips which provide sensory feedback in Chapter 5, but that's a different story...)

The hand exercises coming up are really fundamental for supporting your pencil grip too. They will give you the strength and power in your hands and shoulders and arms that you need to support and strengthen, and steady, the way you hold that pencil.

Another thing you can do pretty easily day to day is to make sure you do lots of things that encourage you to use the tripod grasp pattern: cutting with scissors, using tweezers to pick up small items, buttoning, zippering, etc.

Using smaller writing utensils can also trick your fingers into making a tripod grasp: why don't you break some crayons into small pieces or use a golf pencil? This forces you to place your fingers close to the tip, improving control during writing and improving your grasp as well.

But ALL the activities in the different chapters of this book will support you to be more relaxed about writing and to have fun with writing, and you never know, your grip may just follow along.

Quiz: What's Your Writing-Learning Style?

Answer the following questions, either on your own, or with a helpful grown-up. Tick the boxes that apply to you. For your results and next steps, look at the "Quiz results and next steps" section that follows the quiz.

1. You are sitting on the rug. Your teacher just announced that it is now writing workshop. What is your first thought?

   a. "Ugh. My eyes are hurting already." ☐

   b. "I don't know how my hands are going to write all of those words." ☐

   c. "How long are we supposed to do this?" ☐

   d. "Do we have to sit up and do this the whole entire time? My body feels tired already." ☐

   e. "How am I going to do my work with all of this noise?" ☐

2. You begin writing. Uh oh...

   a. The lines are getting blurry. ☐

   b. Your hand is getting tired. ☐

   c. You forgot what you were going to write. ☐

   d. You just need to lay your head down—it's too hard to hold your body up. ☐

   e. It is just too noisy, there are too many people around you to do your writing! ☐

3. You would say that your biggest problem as a writer is...

   a. Keeping your eyes on the page: ☐
- keeping letters on the line
- keeping spacing between words.

   b. Forming letters: ☐
- writing hard enough
- writing enough lines or pages of text.

   c. Losing track of your thoughts when you write: ☐
- writing as quickly as your mind is going
- keeping your thoughts on your work.

   d. Sitting up in your chair when you write: ☐
- following multiple steps when you write
- remembering the right and left sides of your body.

   e. Staying within your space: ☐
- keeping out extra noises and stuff you can see in the room when writing
- not becoming too frustrated if writing becomes too challenging.

QUIZ RESULTS AND NEXT STEPS

If you answered mostly a's...

You may be affected by "Helping Your Eyes Out" difficulties. Go to Chapter 2 to learn more about what this means, as well as to find strategies in this area to help writing feel easier and in your control.

If you answered mostly b's...

You may be affected by "When Your Hands Just Feel Tired" difficulties. Go to Chapter 3 to learn more about what this means, as well as to find strategies in this area to help writing feel easier and in your control.

If you answered mostly c's...

You may be affected by "When it's Hard to Focus" difficulties. Go to Chapter 4 to learn more about what this means, as well as to find strategies in this area to help writing feel easier and in your control.

If you answered mostly d's...

You may be affected by "Big Body Stuff" difficulties. Go to Chapter 1 to learn more about what this means, as well as to find strategies in this area to help writing feel easier and in your control.

If you answered mostly e's...

You may be affected by "When All Your Body's Feelings and Senses Get Too Much (or Too Little)" difficulties. Go to Chapter 5 to learn more about what this means, as well as to find strategies in this area to help writing feel easier and in your control.

Now, let's get ready to delve into your just-right strategies that you have discovered based on this quiz. You may find that you have checked off a mixture of letters. You can go to all chapters, but I would suggest starting out in the chapter with the most letters checked.

Before We Begin! A Fun Exercise for Before, During, and After Writing

Here's a neat hand exercise routine that you can do anywhere—on your own, with a grown-up, in your class. Practice in the car or when you're watching TV!

It will make your hands stronger, and loosen up any tired muscles. It's a bit like when you warm up your body for P.E., baseball, or dance!

It's especially useful when you are about to begin writing—and when you need a break from writing before you start up again.

And the best bit? It only takes about two minutes!

Look at the pictures showing how Joel, Kwame, Lucy, and Sasha—who you'll meet again throughout this book—are doing the exercises in the sequence, and copy them.

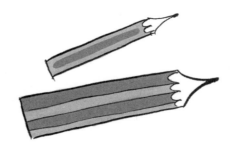

HAND WARM-UP EXERCISE

1. Copy Joel: Shake out both hands.

2. Copy Kwame: Open and close both hands 5–10 times.

3. Copy Lucy: Press palms together and hold for 10 seconds.

4. Copy Sasha: Seat push up: with flat palms and feet planted on the floor, push up from your chair and hold for 10 seconds.

MY HAND WARM-UP STAR CHART

Give yourself a sticker or draw a star in the boxes below each time you managed the routine!

I did my hand warm-up exercises!

CHAPTER 1

Let's Learn Some Writing Strategies for Big Body Stuff

LET'S TALK ABOUT HOW BIG BODY STUFF CAN MAKE WRITING TRICKY

Did you try out the Hand Warm-Up Exercise? Good job! Now I'm going to tell you something about me, when I was little! I was the kid who always needed to look at the other students when the teacher gave a direction, to copy what they were doing.

Always.

If she told us more than one thing to do at once? Forget it! Even when I looked to my classmates, I was lost!

That definitely made me feel nervous. The problem was, I was not great at: a) telling helpful grown-ups how I was feeling, or b) asking for help.

I think that's why I love what I do in my job. It's why I encourage kids to figure out what strategies work best for them, so that you guys will be able to speak up and advocate for yourself, talking to grown-ups and others around you to get what you need to learn best.

But enough of me! I could tell you more about my school days, but that's a whole entire other story for a different time.

This chapter was written for you if your body feels, well, difficult to manage at times. Hard to coordinate.

Maybe you have trouble remembering your right side and left side. Or holding yourself up without a chair when you sit on the rug.

You may be like me, and get confused when you have to follow lots of steps.

Don't worry. Try out the exercises and tools laid out on the next pages.

So here you are. Take that control back. You've got this!

LIST OF KIT YOU WILL NEED (ASK A GROWN-UP TO HELP YOU FIND THESE ITEMS!)

Note: This is merely a suggested list. While many items can be found online, I suggest trying to use what you have in your school or at home first and go from there. Be creative.

1. Something to use as a foot stool

2. A variety of pencils in different shapes and sizes

3. Wedge Cushion

4. Gel-Filled Cushion

5. Trace the 8

6. Wrist Cross Ankle Cross

7. Feel My Body

LAUREN'S MENU OF WRITING STRATEGIES FOR BIG BODY STUFF

Foot Stool

A foot stool is any object placed under your feet so that they don't hang under your seat! This tool can help you feel where your body is when you write, helping you focus. Examples of objects that you can use include a crate, a cardboard box, or a large block.

Let's try using this tool out as we practice writing a word out on the lines below, shall we?

Write the word "Silly." How did that feel?

Let's get writing!

Pencil Choice

Different types of pencils help different writers! You may find that you like thicker pencils if they feel that they are easier to grip, or you may prefer golf pencils. Other kids may like mechanical pencils!

Let's test out this tool! Try out a variety of different pencils.

Write out these words on the lines below "Kids need more recess!"

Was that better? Which pencil felt best?

Let's get writing!

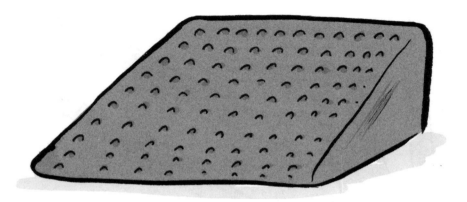

Wedge Cushion

A disc air-filled wedge cushion provides what we call "vestibular" movement (up and down or spinning). Something great about these kinds of seats for you kiddos who have trouble sitting up (I can relate to that, since I am always working on my posture, right Mom?) is that they help you to sit more upright. Sitting up helps your brain and body feel more awake!

Let's write out the word "Happy" on the lines below.

Let's get writing!

Gel-Filled Cushion

A gel-filled cushion allows you to feel more stable while you sit. If your core (belly) feels tired often, this type of cushion can help you sit upright for longer periods! This is different from a wedge cushion, which actually looks kind of like a triangle. A wedge cushion pushes your hips forward, helping you sit upright. A gel cushion is not inflated, and makes it easier to balance if you have difficulty maintaining your balance. This cushion can then improve body awareness, which can then help you focus on your writing.

Ready to use this one?

Ok, let's try out this sentence on the lines below "Cushions are comfy."

Let's get writing!

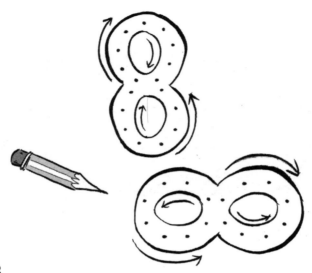

Trace the 8

Picture an 8 lying on its side. Pretend that you've drawn it! Picture how it looks, and imagine it's right there in front of you. Take your right hand (using your shoulder as well!) and trace it carefully. Now, trace over it with your left hand (remember, using your whole arm including your shoulder!). Now, take both hands together (one fist on top of the other) and trace over the 8 using both your hands together.

Use the line below to write whatever words you like. Or just doodle and make some fun patterns... Did you know an 8 on its side is the infinity sign?

Let's get writing!

Wrist Cross Ankle Cross

Does your teacher have you do exercises where you cross one side of your body to the next? Confused? When you take one part of your body and cross it to the oppose side of your body, this gives your brain really strong information by connecting its two hemispheres, or sides. This exercise also uses what we call proprioceptive input (deep pressure to the joints of the body). In this way, the exercise allows you to feel where your body is. Directions:

1. Stand up.
2. Cross your right ankle over your left ankle and plant your feet. Press them together.
3. Cross your left wrist over your right wrist. Press them together.
4. Hold this position for 10 seconds.
5. Switch.

Right. Sit back down at your writing space now and write out "I am so focused!" on the lines below.

Let's get writing!

Feel My Body

This one sounds kinda strange, doesn't it? It feels obvious that you should know where your body is at all times, no? Guess what? If you are super tired or really stressed, you can lose track of where different parts of your body are, which then affects, well, everything! "Feel My Body" is an exercise that forces one part of your body to cross to the other side, forcing the two sides of your brain to chat—improving focus! Directions:

1. Lean down in your chair. Cross your arms.
2. Take your left ankle with your right hand, and your right ankle with your left hand. Squeeze firmly, and say "Ankles."
3. Repeat, with arms crossed, to your knees, hips, and shoulders.

Let's write the word "Hemispheres."
on the lines below.

Let's get writing!

_____

. . . .

_____

_____

. . . .

_____

How did that go?

Amazing job trying all of your strategies! Now that you have tried out each strategy, you can think about how they felt.

Did any single strategy really stand out for you? Let's go through each one together.

On the next page, put a circle next to the emoji that represents which one felt best for you at this first go-around.

You should use the one/s that feel best most frequently, because they are the ones that work for you!

Look at all of the strategies with a smiley face—those are your go-to strategies to try out. These are the first strategies you should enter into your Tracking My Progress chart, which you will also find below. And those smiley face strategies are the ones you can use during writing at home and at school. It's time to be super independent—just like we talked about earlier in this book, remember?

Tracking My Progress is a really helpful chart to help you keep track of each of the big body strategies you used from this chapter, including how often you use them, and how helpful you find them.

Remember...

★ The more often you use each chosen strategy, making sure you do it the same each time, the more helpful it will be.
★ Don't just say "this won't work" about a strategy. Try it first. Give it a fair chance (that means more than once).
★ Use all strategies the right way. Ask a grown-up to check with you at first.

1. Foot Stool (p.26)

2. Pencil Choice (p.27)

3. Wedge Seat Cushion (p.28)

4. Gel-Filled Cushion (p.29)

5. Trace the 8 (p.30)

6. Wrist Cross Ankle Cross (p.31)

7. Feel My Body (p.32)

TRACKING MY PROGRESS CHART

Check out the chart below. It was made with you in mind to best help you figure out which strategies help you to get your writing "just right." Get it?

   Here's the thing. It's very important that you be super responsible and independent in filling out this chart on your own, without a grown-up. It's ok to need their support at first, to get in the swing of things. As you get used to how the chart works, the easier it will be to complete it independently—on your own!

Instructions

★ Which strategies have you chosen to do your best writing? Add them to the chart.
★ Each time you use these strategies at home or school, note the date and time that you used them. How helpful were the strategies in making your writing easier/more successful?
★ How many sentences/words/pages did you write?
★ Draw the emoji on the chart to show how you felt using the strategy (these are shown at the top of the chart).

Note: It will be super helpful to look at what you write over the course of time (even over a week!) to really see what helps you the most!

Tracking My Progress: Big Body Stuff

Strategy choice	Date and time strategy used	# Words/Sentences/ Pages	How I felt using the strategy (draw)

CHAPTER 2

Let's Learn Some Writing Strategies for Helping Your Eyes Out

Hand Warm-Up Exercise

1. Shake out both hands.

2. Open and close both hands 5–10 times.

3. Press palms together and hold for 10 seconds.

4. Seat push up: with flat palms and feet planted on the floor, push up from your chair and hold for 10 seconds.

LET'S TALK ABOUT *HOW* HELPING YOUR EYES OUT CAN MAKE WRITING EASIER

Have you done your hand warm-up exercises? Great job. Give yourself a sticker or draw yourself a star in the chart on page 22.

Now, did you know that your eyes are a muscle?

That's right. And they get tired and worn out, just like your legs and arms do. Maybe even more so. I'll explain.

Reading? Your eyes.

Writing? Yep, that too.

Focusing on your teacher. Check. Making eye contact when talking? Looking at the ball during gym? Looking where you are going when you are walking? Video games? TV? Check, check, check.

Some people's eyes are bothered more than others. And that is ok.

Hard to see the line when writing? Lose your place when you read? Do your eyes feel teary or do objects get blurred when you try to read or focus on something close by or far away?

If any of this sounds like you, why not give the writing strategies in this chapter a try and give your eyes a rest?

So here you are. Take that control back. You've got this!

LIST OF KIT YOU WILL NEED (ASK A GROWN-UP TO HELP YOU FIND THESE ITEMS!)

1. Different kinds of paper

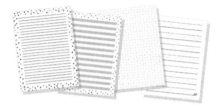

2. I-Spy Bean Bags

3. Mirror Me Moves

4. Eye Break

5. Eye Scans

6. Pencil with eraser

7. Three-inch binder or lever arch folder (labeled My Eye Muscle Workbook)

8. Three-inch binder or lever arch folder (labeled My Reversals Workbook)

HELPING YOUR EYES OUT STRATEGIES

Fun Paper Choices

Just like my favorite food is definitely hot dogs, your favorite food may be Brussels sprouts! Guess what? It's the same thing with paper choice! Some kids write better on certain colors/backgrounds of paper. Other kids may like writing on extra-large lines. I've worked with students who love writing on graph paper.

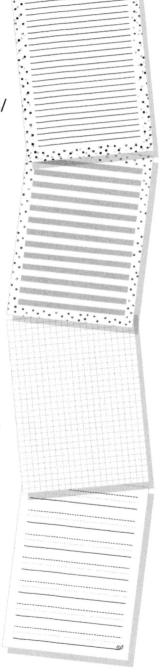

Find out what works for you by trying different types of paper and comparing the results. You can find your own notebooks and paper styles.

And check out the fun sample paper choices below.

We've provided four different types of paper here. Full size sheets are available in Appendix 3 at the back of the book, or you can ask a grown-up to print more off for you.

Note that you will see that two of the paper types look exactly the same! You should color in these colored papers using a highlighter pen or coloring pencil of your choice—before you write on it!

Let's try writing out this sentence on each of the four kinds of paper: "Kids should play outside more often."

Which paper is easiest to write on? Which paper makes your writing neatest?

I-Spy Bean Bags

An I-Spy Bean Bag is created out of a pencil case filled with small objects, including magnetic fridge letters and beads. You can even include small toys! This activity is a fun tool to help you strengthen your eyes and brain as you search for sight words that your class is working on. For example, if a sight word is "the," you can look for the letters t-h-e! Follow this with writing the word t-h-e as a nice way to strengthen your eyes as you search for each letter, while also working on your handwriting.

Write the word "The" on the lines below.

Let's get writing!

Mirror Me Moves

Pretend that your teacher or parent is in the mirror, and you are their reflection—would you go faster, slower? You would move at exactly the same speed, right? You would also only move the same parts of your body! Ask your helpful grown-up to assist you with this exercise. Copy their moves, just like a mirror. This activity helps connect your eyes, brain, and body, as they have to speak to each other to do the movement correctly!

Let's write "Copy my moves" on the lines below.

Let's get writing!

_____

_____

_____

_____

_____

Eye Break

Did you know that the eyes are a muscle and they definitely get tired with all the focusing that they do throughout the day! If you feel as if your eyes are bothering you before or during writing, this is a good time to do this exercise. It helps your eyes take a well-deserved break! Directions:

1. Rub your hands together until they feel warm.
2. Close your eyes.
3. Place your warmed palms over your closed eyes. Hold for at least 10 seconds.
4. To increase focus, cross your arms before placing them over your eyes.

Let's write the word "Rest" on the lines below.

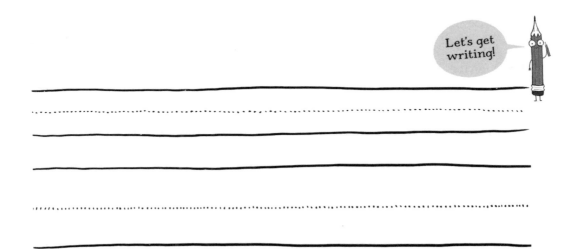

Let's get writing!

Eye Scans

This exercise helps you strengthen your eye muscles. This is important—your eye muscles help you to keep your letters on the lines, and remember the spaces in between words! Another name for this exercise is saccades (you pronounce it "s'kades"), which is when your eyes move quickly from side to side, left to right. How fast can you go? This is an important skill to use when you are reading, too! Directions:

1. Keep your head straight—only move your eyes!
2. Look at the smiley face.
3. Look at the check mark.
4. Repeat five times.

Let's get writing!

Let's write "Left to right" on the lines below.

Pencil to Nose

This super fun exercise is another great way to help you strengthen your eye muscles, which are really important for helping you keep your letters on the lines, and get your spacing right in between words! The name of the movement that your eyes are doing with this exercise is "convergence," when you bring your eyes together. This is also an important skill during reading. Directions:

1. Keep your head straight—you are only moving your eyes!
2. Pick up a pencil, and turn it upside down so that you are looking at the eraser.
3. Hold the pencil at an arm's-length away, pointing at the middle of your body (at your nose).
4. Slowly, slowly, bring the pencil towards your nose (without touching it), staring at the eraser.

Let's get writing!

Let's write "Pencil to nose" on the lines below.

My Eye Muscle Workbook

This is a slightly different kind of activity. It's something you need to create, over time, with the assistance of your helpful grown-up.

You will need a three-inch binder. You're going to fill it with a bunch of fun activities that help build the muscles of your eyes and connect them to your hands. This includes stuff like connect the dots, mazes, and word searches.

There are some examples in Appendix 3 at the back of the book.

You could find some fun ones of your own online or in coloring and activity books too.

Put them into a binder, then you can go back to it whenever you have a few minutes to spare.

Give the binder a label. You can call it your "Eye Muscle Workbook." Make it your own by decorating it with your favorite things (I love stickers, personally!).

Pick one to three pages to do from your binder before you do a class writing or homework activity, each time, as a warm-up.

Guess what? You can turn your binder on its side and use it as a slantboard, too. This will help if your hand starts to hurt when you write, since you can rest your wrist on the slant, instead of holding it in the air.

Let's try out a page now, shall we?

Let's try the maze!

My Reversals Workbook

For this activity, you need to use a three-inch binder (or lever arch folder).

You can fill the binder with activities, including the ones in this book. And print some out of your own, too.

Hmm, you may wonder, what are reversals?

Reversals are when you write a letter backwards. This can be totally normal, and often happens to kids. Your Reversals Workbook is a binder with laminated pages of reversals, which are letters and numbers that you have been having trouble forming the right way round. That's ok! The more you practice writing them, the easier it will be to put them into what we therapists call "muscle memory"—ah, another big therapist word! Muscle memory is a fancy way of explaining the process of when your body completes a movement automatically without thinking through practice.

Think about riding a bike—you haven't ridden all year because it's been cold, but as soon as spring comes you jump on the seat and start riding right away. That's muscle memory!

Use your reversals binder before you do a writing activity.

Guess what? You can turn it on its side and use it as a slantboard, too! This will help if your hand starts to hurt when you write, since you can rest your wrist on the slant, instead of holding it in the air.

Let's practice a page!

Directions: Find and circle the b's.

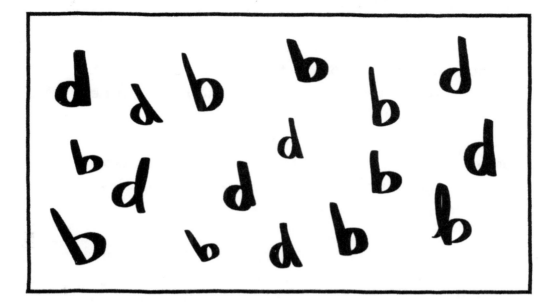

How many b's did you find?

Find the d's.

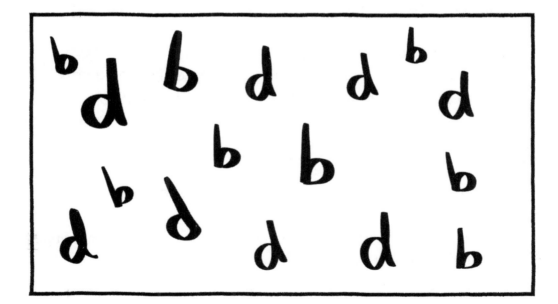

How many d's did you find?

HOW DID THAT GO?

Amazing job trying all of your strategies! Now that you have tried out each strategy, you can think about how they felt.

Did any single strategy really stand out for you? Let's go through each one together.

On the next page, put a circle next to the emoji that represents which one felt best for you at this first go-around.

You should use the one/s that feel best most frequently, because they are the ones that work for you!

Look at all of the strategies with a smiley face—those are your go-to strategies to try out. These are the first strategies you should enter into your Tracking My Progress chart, which you will also find below. And those smiley face strategies are the ones you can use during writing at home and at school. It's time to be super independent—just like we talked about earlier in this book, remember?

Tracking My Progress is a really helpful chart to help you keep track of each strategy you use from this chapter, including how often you use them, and how effective you find them.

Remember...

* ★ The more consistently you use each chosen strategy, the more potentially helpful it will be.
* ★ Don't just say "this won't work" about a strategy. Try it first. Give it a fair chance (that means more than once).
* ★ Use all strategies the right way.

1. Fun Paper Choices (p.40)

2. I-Spy Bean Bags (p.41)

3. Mirror Me Moves (p.42)

4. Eye Break (p.43)

5. Eye Scans (p.44)

6. Pencil to Nose (p.45)

7. My Eye Muscle Workbook (p.46)

8. My Reversals Workbook (p.48)

TRACKING MY PROGRESS CHART

Check out the chart below. It was made with you in mind to best help you figure out which strategies help you to get your writing "just right." Get it?

Here's the thing. It's very important that you be super responsible and independent in filling out this chart on your own, without a grown-up. It's ok to need their support at first, to get in the swing of things. As you get used to how the chart works, the easier it will be to complete it independently—on your own!

Instructions

★ Which strategies have you chosen to do your best writing? Add them to the chart.
★ Each time you use these strategies at home or school, note the date and time that you used them. How helpful were the strategies in making your writing easier/more successful?
★ How many sentences/words/pages did you write?
★ Draw the emoji on the chart to show how you felt using the strategy (these are shown at the top of the chart).

Note: It will be super helpful to look at what you write over the course of time (even over a week!) to really see what helps you the most!

Tracking My Progress: Helping Your Eyes Out

Strategy choice	Date and time strategy used	# Words/Sentences/ Pages	How I felt using the strategy (draw)

CHAPTER 3

Let's Learn Some Writing Strategies for When Your Hands Just Feel Tired

Hand Warm-Up Exercise

1. Shake out both hands.

2. Open and close both hands 5–10 times.

3. Press palms together and hold for 10 seconds.

4. Seat push up: with flat palms and feet planted on the floor, push up from your chair and hold for 10 seconds.

*J*ust like our eyes, our hands do a ton of work every day. Think about a typical day in your life.

You wake up. Get dressed—buttons, zippers, shoelaces. They all need your hands!

You eat breakfast too, I assume? My kids are not the biggest fans. (Do you have any breakfast food suggestions, by the way? Feel free to email me. I would love some new ideas.) You pour drinks and open containers and jars of food. Those hands are hard at work yet again!

(And now would be a great time to do your hand warm-ups if you didn't do them already. Done? Good stuff. Give yourself a sticker or a star in the chart earlier in the book.]

Now, let's think about the school day for a second. We immediately think of how much writing you guys do. In fact, the main complaint I get as an occupational therapist is that kids' hands hurt when they write. But guess what? You guys also build, cut, color, paint, glue, sculpt... The list goes on and on.

Oh, and then some of you go home and do homework. Dinner, getting ready for bed. It's a vicious hand-weakening disaster, isn't it?

So, are we in agreement that you guys use your hands a lot?

If you feel your hands getting tired during writing (at home or at school), this chapter is for you!

Let's work together and get those hands strong and make writing a piece of cake!

LIST OF KIT YOU WILL NEED (ASK A GROWN-UP TO HELP YOU FIND THESE ITEMS!)

1. Hand Stamina Exercises Reminder Bookmark

2. Slantboard

3. A variety of cool pencil grips

4. Erasable pens

5. Items for your Motor Tool Box

6. Handwriting Reminder Bookmarks

7. My Handwriting Workbook

WHEN YOUR HANDS JUST FEEL TIRED STRATEGIES

Hand Stamina Exercises Reminder Bookmark

Have you been doing your hand warm-ups from the very start of the book? Good job! Give yourself a big pat on the back and put a sticker in the chart on page 22.

Guess what? As well as warm-ups, you can also use them as writing stamina exercises!

Because the more you practice them, the stronger your hands will get.

In Appendix 2 at the back of the book you'll find bookmarks with the steps on, which your grown-up can laminate for you. You can keep one as a reminder on your desk or pin it to the wall.

I am going to talk about them a bit more here, because they are so great! And the more you practice them, the stronger your hands will get. So you can also think of them as writing stamina exercises!

(Who knows, maybe by the time you get to the end of this book, you will even have learned the sequence off by heart...)

This exercise sequence is perfect for if you have trouble remembering how to form your letters, or if you have difficulty writing your letters neatly, and especially if your hands just feel tired or ache when you write.

Completing this sequence of exercises every day, or a few times a day, can really make a difference!

This is not just an exercise to do before you get writing. You can also do this sequence of hand moves ANY TIME you feel uncomfortable or tired or worried or frustrated during the writing process.

So, here are the steps again:

1. Shake out both hands.

2. Open and close both hands 5–10 times.

3. Press palms together and hold for 10 seconds.

4. Seat push up: with flat palms and feet planted on the floor, push up from your chair, and hold for 10 seconds.

Let's write the word "Hands" on the lines below.

Let's get writing!

Slantboard

Slantboards consist of a sloping writing surface that raises your writing surface so you can see what you are writing more clearly. And, as you write, your wrist is supported, making it easier for your hands to write.

(Tip: a large, three-inch binder works just as well. You can even ask your grown-up assistant to help you glue a clipboard to it, so that papers or books can be attached while you work. Make sure that, whenever you write, there is a binder you can use as a slantboard.)

Let's write the word "Uphill" on the lines below.

Let's get writing!

Pencil Grips

Pencil grips can help your hand hold the pencil correctly, so you feel less tired when you write. They can even give your hand extra tactile (touch) input, so your brain and body connect during the writing process!

Here are some examples of different grips, and how they help:

★ *Foam Grip:* This provides a cushion, so when you write for a long time, your fingers don't hurt as much!

★ *Stetro Grip:* Since this grip is small, it is usually better if you have smaller hands. This pencil even has special indents, or grooves, to guide your fingers into the right position!

★ *Triangle Grip:* Like the name implies, it is shaped like a triangle, and guides your fingers into what we call a tripod (three-finger) grasp.

★ *The Writing CLAW:* This grip really helps kids who have a lot of trouble remembering or figuring an easy way to hold the pencil. It has three loops for the middle, pointer, and thumb to wrap around the pencil.

★ *The Pencil Grip:* This is shaped like a triangle and puts your fingers into that tripod grasp.

★ *The Grotto Grip:* This grip is designed to help you hold the pencil correctly (if your pencil grasp is, well, a little funny!). It even has a guard in the front to prevent the thumb from wrapping over!

The list is probably endless. Experiment, see what is available at your school, local stores, or online, and find a grip that works for you.

Try out the sentence *"I can't wait to go to the park"* on the lines below using whichever grips you have. Which grip made your writing neatest? Which made your hand hurt the least?

Let's get writing!

Erasable Pens

Erasable pens help you to write in a smooth way, and they require less force to get the ink out than ordinary pens, making them a nice choice to use when you find it tricky to write the words hard enough on the paper, or with "firm pressure." They're pretty awesome and fun to use, too.

Let's write "Erase a pen" on the lines below.

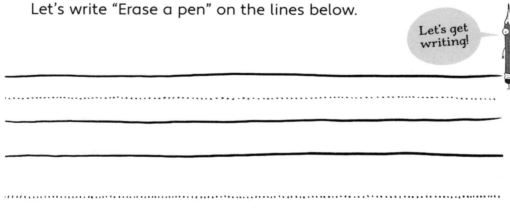

Let's get writing!

Motor Tool Box

A Motor Tool Box is a bin of different fun stuff that helps you build up the strength in the small muscles of your hands. Use items from this box before you begin a writing activity. Examples of objects you can include in your own personal Motor Tool Box are Lego, putty, play dough, and coloring books. When you use these types of objects, you strengthen what we occupational therapists call the "intrinsic" (inside) muscles of the hands—the muscles that are important for writing!

There are some more ideas for what you can include in the appendix. Why don't you ask your grown-up assistant to take a look!

Let's write "Motor toolbox" on the lines below.

Let's get writing!

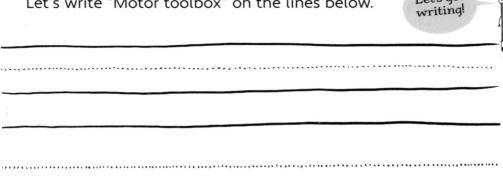

Handwriting Reminder Bookmarks

These are great little bookmarks to keep close by at all times. Or you could pin one on the wall above where you usually write!

These bookmarks are reminders of what to keep in mind each time you go through the writing process. They will jog your memory about what you need to self-check each time you write.

In Appendix 2 at the end of the book there's a template you can laminate and place in your writing center. You could color in this one below!

Before I begin writing...

1. I will write neatly.

2. I will write on the lines.

3. I will put spaces between my words.

4. My letters will be the same size.

5. I will use punctuation and capitalization.

6. I will spell the words I know the best that I can.

7. If I need a re-focuser, I can do so from my seat and get back to work.

8. If I am feeling like I really have to move, I can ask my teacher for a quick two-minute standing exercise break.

Before I begin writing...

1. I will write neatly.

2. I will write on the lines.
   Aa Bb

3. I will put spaces between my words.
   I can put spaces!

4. My letters will be the same size.
   Hello

5. I will use punctuation and capitalization.
   Do you want to get some pizza, David?

6. I will spell the words I know the best that I can.
   Sight words

7. If I need a re-focuser, I can do so from my seat and get back to work.

8. If I am feeling like I really have to move, I can ask my teacher for a quick two-minute standing exercise break.

My Handwriting Workbook

We like binders in this guide, don't we? Just like we talked about the reversals binder and the eye muscles binder in the last chapter, here we are introducing a handwriting binder! This is a folder with laminated pages of letters and numbers in upper and lower case letters. The more you practice writing them, the easier it will be to put them into what we therapists call "muscle memory," where forming the letters correctly feels simple, as you have practiced it so often!

Use the binder before you do a writing activity.

Why don't you give it a super silly name, that shows it's uniquely yours (like "Hairy Handwriting Hype")?

Guess what? You can turn it on its side and use it as a slantboard, too.

Check out Appendix 3 at the back of the book to work on your handwriting (it's not boring, I'm telling you!).

Let's write the name for your handwriting workbook on the lines below.

Let's get writing!

HOW DID THAT GO?

Amazing job trying all of your strategies! Now that you have tried out each strategy, how did they feel?

Did any single strategy really stand out for you? Let's go through each one together.

On the next page, put a circle next to the emoji that represents which one felt best at this first go-around.

The one/s that feel best should be used most frequently, along with the chart provided at the end of this chapter.

Look at all of the strategies with a smiley face—those are your go-to strategies to try out. These are the first strategies you should enter into your chart, which you will also find below. And those smiley face strategies are the ones you can use during writing at home and at school. It's time to be super independent— just like we talked about earlier in this book, remember?

Tracking My Progress is a really helpful chart to help you keep track of each strategy you use from this chapter, including how often you use them, and how effective you find them.

Remember...

★ The more consistently you use each chosen strategy, the more potentially helpful it will be.
★ Don't just say "this won't work" about a strategy. Try it first. Give it a fair chance (that means more than once).
★ Use all strategies the right way.

1. Hand Stamina Exercises (p.58)

2. Slantboard (p.59)

3. Pencil Grips (p.60)

4. Erasable Pens (p.62)

5. Motor Tool Box (p.63)

6. Handwriting Reminder Bookmarks (p.64)

7. My Handwriting Workbook (p.65)

TRACKING MY PROGRESS CHART

Check out the chart below. It was made with you in mind to best help you figure out which strategies help you to get your writing "just right." Get it?

Here's the thing. It's very important that you be super responsible and independent in filling out this chart on your own, without a grown-up. It's ok to need their support at first, to get in the swing of things. As you get used to how the chart works, the easier it will be to complete it independently—on your own!

Instructions

★ Which strategies have you chosen to do your best writing? Add them to the chart.

★ Each time you use these strategies at home or school, note the date and time that you used them. How helpful were the strategies in making your writing easier/more successful?

★ How many sentences/words/pages did you write?

★ Draw the emoji on the chart to show how you felt using the strategy (these are shown at the top of the chart).

Note: It will be super helpful to look at what you write over the course of time (even over a week!) to really see what helps you the most!

Tracking My Progress: When Your Hands Just Feel Tired

Strategy choice	Date and time strategy used	# Words/Sentences/Pages	How I felt using the strategy (draw)

CHAPTER 4

Let's Learn Some Writing Strategies for When it's Hard to Focus

Hand Warm-Up Exercise

1. Shake out both hands.

2. Open and close both hands 5–10 times.

3. Press palms together and hold for 10 seconds.

4. Seat push up: with flat palms and feet planted on the floor, push up from your chair and hold for 10 seconds.

"Focus! Concentrate!" Have you heard that as you've thought about an exciting play date when you were, erm, supposed to be writing about apples, or during homework when instead you were talking to your parents about your favorite type of cake?

I mean, it happens. Sometimes.

But some kids have trouble keeping their mind focused on their work for lots of their day, especially when it comes to writing.

Because writing can feel like a lot.

You may have the idea in your brain, but your hands aren't writing fast enough to keep up!

Or, you may think of an idea, but you can't stop other thoughts from popping up in your brain!

You may have had an idea...and you were writing about the idea for a few minutes, but then you just lost focus after a bit.

This chapter is full of strategies to help you keep those amazing ideas in your brain *and* get them onto paper. That way you get to share them with the people you care about!

You'll see that some of them are pretty neat—like sitting on a big ball! Or wearing special headphones in class or at home. Maybe don't do those two things at once though...well, I guess it's up to you!

LIST OF KIT YOU WILL NEED (ASK A GROWN-UP TO HELP YOU FIND THESE ITEMS!)

1. Soft 2B Pencils

2. Yoga Ball/Yoga Ball Chair

3. Metronome/Metronome App

4. Visual Timer

5. Noise-Reducing Headphones

6. Visual Blocking Folder

7. Toe Touch Cross

WHEN IT'S HARD TO FOCUS STRATEGIES

Soft 2B Pencils

Do you feel as if you need to *write quickly* to get your ideas out? A good pencil for this is a soft 2B pencil. Originally designed for drawing and sketching, this type of pencil allows you to write more smoothly, and tends to be less tiring on your hands.

A really great but quite expensive brand is the Bazic variety. But any 2B pencil will do. They're easier to write with, and easier to erase, than traditional HB pencils are.

Let's write "Soft pencil" on the lines below.

Let's get writing!

_____

. . . .

_____

. . . .

_____

Yoga Ball/Yoga Chair

This is a fun one to try!
This special type of chair is
like a big ball, and if you're
the kind of person who often feels
wriggly and has trouble sitting still, it allows you to get out
excess energy from a seated position. While if you often feel the
opposite—slow and tired—it will help you wake up your brain
and body. You can sit on the ball at your desk. Ask a grown-up
to help you position it.

Let's write "Yoga ball" on the lines below.

Let's get writing!

Metronome

Completing your writing activities in time to a metronome can support you with your focus and attention. The steady and consistent rhythm helps your brain and body stay on task. Pick the metronome speed that works best for you.

Let's write "I can write to the beat" on the lines below.

Let's get writing!

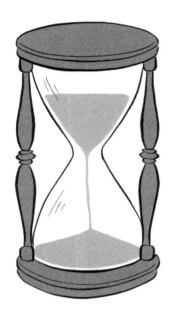

Visual Timer

Set the timer for however long you expect that you can sit. Not sure? A good estimate is one minute per year of your life. So if you are eight years old, you can sit for at least eight minutes and write. Knowing how long you are expected to sit (especially when you are doing something that's challenging for you) can make it easier for you to focus! Not long to go now...!

Let's write the word "Time" on the lines below.

Let's get writing!

Noise-Reducing Headphones

Do you get easily distracted by your friends talking, or even by the sound of other kids' chairs scraping? Or your kid brother playing with his toys? Try using noise-reducing headphones to help you focus on your own work, and to help you tune out the noises around you!

Let's write the word "Quiet" on the lines below.

Let's get writing!

Visual Blocking Folder

Is it hard for you to focus when there is too much to look at? All you need to do to create your own "office" is to place your folder—maybe one of your workbooks you've made in Chapter 3 or 4—open and on its side, in front of you, to create a blank "wall" effect! Neat, huh?

Let's write the word "Private office" on the lines below.

Let's get writing!

Toe Touch Cross

This simple whole-body exercise provides you with something we occupational therapists call crossed midline input! That means it allows the two sides of your brain to connect. It also provides vestibular input (the vestibular system is our balance system) because your head goes below the level of your heart, which is very calming to the body.

Being focused and calm, while feeling your body, is essential to being able to get your ideas on paper. This is a great exercise to do before you start writing, especially if you have issues with staying focused. Directions:

1. Standing up, start with your legs shoulder width apart.
2. Spread your arms out.
3. Cross your right arm and reach it across your midsection to touch your left foot.
4. Repeat on the other side.

Let's write the word "Touch your toes" on the lines below.

Let's get writing!

HOW DID THAT GO?

Amazing job trying all of your strategies! Now that you have tried out each strategy, how did they feel? Did any single strategy really stand out for you?

Let's go through each one together.

On the next page, put a circle next to the emoji that represents which one felt best at this first go-around.

The one/s that feel best should be used most frequently, along with the chart provided at the end of this chapter.

Look at all of the strategies with a smiley face—those are your go-to strategies to try out with your chart, and use during writing at home and at school. It's time to be super independent— just like we talked about earlier in this book, remember?

Tracking My Progress is a really helpful chart to help you keep track of each strategy you use from this chapter, including how often you use them, and how effective you find them.

Remember...

★ The more consistently you use each chosen strategy, the more potentially helpful it will be.
★ Don't just say "this won't work" about a strategy. Try it first. Give it a fair chance (that means more than once).
★ Use all strategies the right way.

1. Soft 2B Pencils (p.73)

2. Yoga Ball/Yoga Chair (p.74)

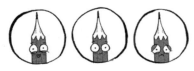

3. Metronome (p.75)

4. Visual Timer (p.76)

5. Noise-Reducing Headphones (p.77)

6. Visual Blocking Folder (p.78)

7. Toe Touch Cross (p.79)

TRACKING MY PROGRESS CHART

Check out the chart below. It was made with you in mind to best help you figure out which strategies help you to get your writing "just right." Get it?

Here's the thing. It's very important that you be super responsible and independent in filling out this chart on your own, without a grown-up. It's ok to need their support at first, to get in the swing of things. As you get used to how the chart works, the easier it will be to complete it independently—on your own!

Instructions

★ Which strategies have you chosen to do your best writing? Add them to the chart.
★ Each time you use these strategies at home or school, note the date and time that you used them. How helpful were the strategies in making your writing easier/more successful?
★ How many sentences/words/pages did you write?
★ Draw the emoji on the chart to show how you felt using the strategy (these are shown at the top of the chart).

Note: It will be super helpful to look at what you write over the course of time (even over a week!) to really see what helps you the most!

Tracking My Progress: When It's Hard to Focus

Strategy choice	Date and time strategy used	# Words/Sentences/ Pages	How I felt using the strategy (draw)

CHAPTER 5

Let's Learn Some Writing Strategies for When All Your Body's Feelings and Senses Get Too Much (or Too Little)

Hand Warm-Up Exercise

1. Shake out both hands.

2. Open and close both hands 5–10 times.

3. Press palms together and hold for 10 seconds.

4. Seat push up: with flat palms and feet planted on the floor, push up from your chair and hold for 10 seconds.

You know the assignment. You have the paper. You have a sharpened pencil. You are good to go, pencil poised.

Scratch, your neighbor's pencil marks the paper. You block it out, and return to your work.

Stomp, stomp, the little kids in kindergarten are walking past the classroom, heading out to recess. Lucky them!

You're not looking forward to your own recess anyhow, because yesterday you had a big row with your best friend.

Someone scrapes their chair back in your class, and the noise grinds into your ears.

Suddenly, a flash of colors of posters and paintings hanging from the ceiling floods your eyes. Your neighbor is too close, her paper and folder are suffocating you.

You look again at your classmates. Everyone else seems to be working diligently on their writing.

You forget what you were supposed to be doing. You are frozen and want to run all at once.

Can you relate to this feeling? I certainly can, since I often experienced it as a kid. When I was faced with math activities, it often made me feel these complicated feelings even more.

By the way, did you do your hand warm-up exercises lately? Why don't you do them now, before we get started on this chapter?

Great job. Go back and give yourself a sticker for the chart on page 22 of this book. Or you could draw yourself a star or other cool shape.

Ok, so this chapter is full of fun strategies to support you in keeping those amazing ideas in your brain as you write, even when life feels too much!

So, take control over those yucky or confusing feelings, and those intense sensations, and get that writing done!

LIST OF KIT YOU WILL NEED (ASK A GROWN-UP TO HELP YOU FIND THESE ITEMS!)

1. Sensory bins

5. Velcro Dots

2. Shoulder Press

6. Spiky Pencil Grip

3. Play Dough Writing

7. Weighted Pencil Grip

4. Head Below Knees

8. Mantra

WHEN ALL YOUR BODY'S FEELINGS AND SENSES GET TOO MUCH (OR TOO LITTLE) STRATEGIES

Sensory Bin Writing

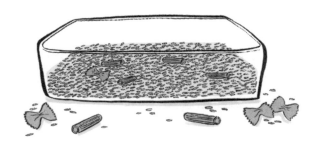

A sensory bin is a tub, bowl, or tray full of stuff like rice, moonsand, noodles, or beans. You or your helpful grown-up can choose which. Or you could try different things on different days.

Now practice writing letters, numbers, or words with your fingers in the tub filled with that rice, moonsand, noodles, or those dried beans (maybe not baked beans...)! This activity helps you remember what you write since it adds that important tactile/touch experience, getting the letter and number shapes into your muscle memory!

This activity can also just be a nice thing to do! It gives you a sensory break, like a change of scene for when your hands get bored of writing all the time. It's a great strategy to use if your body is feeling wiggly or your mind is becoming overwhelmed.

Let's write "Feeling letters" on the lines below.

Let's get writing!

Shoulder Press

This simple exercise is a bit like giving yourself a reassuring hug! You can do this when you're sitting at your desk, any time things get a bit too much. We occupational therapists know the reason it feels so great is that it gives you important deep pressure input.

It is also an exercise where you are crossing the midline (one side of your body crosses to the other), allowing the two sides of your brain to connect, which can make you feel calmer and more settled inside.

Reach both your hands across your middle making an "x" shape. Press them firmly on opposite shoulders. Hold, for at least ten seconds. Switch the arm that's on top and repeat.

Let's write "Big hug" on the lines below.

Let's get writing!

Play Dough Writing

Try creating letters, numbers, or even sight words or sentences out of play dough. Rolling, squeezing, and forming the letters out of play dough can really help you remember the direction of how the letter or number is formed, and even the order of how to write the sight word you are trying to write, since it adds that important tactile/touch aspect, getting

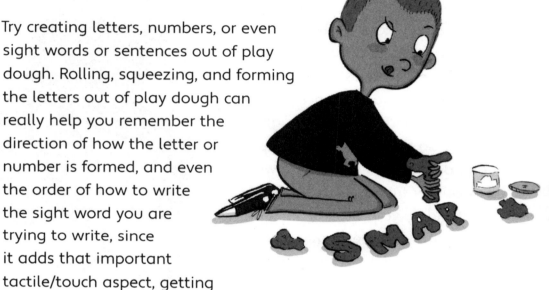

what you practice into your muscle memory! This can also be a nice sensory break, as well, if your body is feeling wiggly or your mind is becoming overwhelmed.

Let's write "Play dough" on the lines below.

Let's get writing!

Head Below Knees

This exercise incorporates that important vestibular system input (remember, your vestibular system is what helps you balance and keep your head and body in the right place!). So this activity can help you calm down if you are feeling worried, anxious, or frustrated.

Stand by your desk or writing table with your feet firmly planted on the floor, slightly spreading your knees apart. Now, reach your head down between your knees, letting your arms hang at your sides, for at least five seconds. (It is important to come up slowly to avoid getting dizzy.)

Let's write "Do you see your toes" on the lines below.

Let's get writing!

Velcro Dots

You can stick two little circles of Velcro onto your pencil, one with a smooth texture and one with a rough texture. Try switching between the soft and rough circles—the contrast for your fingertips will really wake you up and make you feel more alert. And it helps you to concentrate. The circles provide great tactile (touch) input, and adding them to your pencil is a great way to keep calm and write on!

Let's write "Smooth and scratchy" on the lines below.

Let's get writing!

Spiky Pencil Grip

We've seen some great pencil grips in the previous chapter. Occupational therapists love pencil grips! The spiky pencil grip is a special kind of grip that provides great tactile (touch) sensory input for kids who like to touch things, even during writing. Do you press extra hard when you write? This type of pencil grip may also help you press less hard since you are getting that touch input into your hands.

Let's write the word "Spiky" on the lines below.

Let's get writing!

Weighted Pencil Grip

This is a grip that's great if you feel that things can all get too much when you're writing. A weighted pencil grip will provide you with awesome proprioceptive feedback. Do you press too hard when you write? This weighted grip may help you press less hard with the pencil too. It can help you get more control of your writing by making you more aware of your hands as you write. The added weight to your pencil also makes this a calming tool to use if you begin to feel stressed as you write.

Let's write the word "Heavy" on the lines below.

Let's get writing!

"I can do it!"

"I won't give up."

"I am smart."

"I can ask for help."

"I can try another way."

Mantra

Do you sometimes get frustrated, or feel stuck, angry, or worried when you're writing? Saying a mantra can really help. Grown-ups call this positive self-talk.

I get it—writing can definitely feel frustrating sometimes, can't it? Like being stuck in a traffic jam when you really want to get to where you're going. Here are my suggestions for some mantras that you can try to use the next time you are feeling stuck, mad, frustrated, or worried when you are writing.

Which one do you like best? Can you think of some of your own? Write them on the lines below.

Let's get writing!

HOW DID THAT GO?

Amazing job trying all of your strategies! Now that you have tried out each strategy, how did they feel? Did any single strategy really stand out for you?

Let's go through each one together.

On the next page, put a circle next to the emoji that represents which one felt best at this first go-around.

The one/s that feel best should be used most frequently, along with the chart provided at the end of this chapter.

Look at all of the strategies with a smiley face—those are your go-to strategies to try out with your chart, and use during writing at home and at school. It's time to be super independent—just like we talked about earlier in this book, remember?

Tracking My Progress is a really helpful chart to help you keep track of each strategy you use from this chapter, including how often you use them, and how effective you find them.

Remember...

★ The more consistently you use each chosen strategy, the more potentially helpful it will be.

★ Don't just say "this won't work" about a strategy. Try it first. Give it a fair chance (that means more than once).

★ Use all strategies the right way.

1. Sensory Bin Writing (p.87)

2. Shoulder Press (p.88)

3. Play Dough Writing (p.89)

4. Head Below Knees (p.90)

5. Velcro Dots (p.91)

6. Spiky Pencil Grip (p.92)

7. Weighted Pencil Grip (p.93)

8. Mantra (p.94)

TRACKING MY PROGRESS CHART

Check out the chart below. It was made with you in mind to best help you figure out which strategies help you to get your writing "just right." Get it?

    Here's the thing. It's very important that you be super responsible and independent in filling out this chart on your own, without a grown-up. It's ok to need their support at first, to get in the swing of things. As you get used to how the chart works, the easier it will be to complete it independently—on your own!

Instructions

- ★ Which strategies have you chosen to do your best writing? Add them to the chart.
- ★ Each time you use these strategies at home or school, note the date and time that you used them. How helpful were the strategies in making your writing easier/more successful?
- ★ How many sentences/words/pages did you write?
- ★ Draw the emoji on the chart to show how you felt using the strategy (these are shown at the top of the chart).

Note: It will be super helpful to look at what you write over the course of time (even over a week!) to really see what helps you the most!

Tracking My Progress: When All Your Body's Feelings and Senses Get Too Much (or Too Little)

Strategy choice	Date and time strategy used	# Words/Sentences/ Pages	How I felt using the strategy (draw)

PART 2

FOR GROWN-UPS

The Importance of Setting up Writing Routines in School and at Home

Writing is a developmental, whole-body process. It incorporates all the systems of the body, including the visual motor, visual perceptual, fine motor, gross motor, cognitive perceptual, social and emotional, ocular motor, proprioceptive and vestibular, and self-regulation. These systems of the body all need to be working together in this seemingly simple task. No wonder many kids find writing difficult and frustrating, when you think about it. And even if in a child's teenage or adult life they can use a laptop or iPad to write with, they will still always need handwriting for some tasks—ideally, handwriting that other people can read (most of the time!).

Occupational therapy, and work with children who have handwriting issues, whether at home or in an educational setting, has, in the past, leaned towards separate treatment sessions or interventions, that take the child away from the hustle and bustle of family life or the classroom.

However, recent research has proven that the most effective therapeutic work occurs within the child's natural daily environments.

This is the premise of the book you hold in your hands.

As a mom of children who have received special education services, and as a pediatric occupational therapist who provides them (for other children!), I have, on countless occasions, seen not only the value but the ease in which practical interventions can fit into children's daily life.

And guess what? Those practical, made-for-life strategies are the ones I have implemented the most, leading to maximum retention of skills.

Writing is an academic skill, yes. But it is built on a foundation of developmental skills. The chapters in this book, as you work through them with your child, show you how to empower your child to establish the foundational developmental skills they need to write well, comfortably, and in ways that will make homework and classroom time less fraught and frustrating for all concerned.

This is because the activities and strategies in this book are supporting your child to create good habits and routines that underpin the writing process.

In the next pages you will find laminates and other resources that accompany the activities in the book, and suggested sequences (as well as blank templates you can complete with your child). These are all downloadable too from https://libraryjkp. papertrell.com/redeem using the code VYOWUWA.

At-a-Glance Desk Reminders

These are menus of the activities in the book that you can photocopy or download at home or at school, then laminate, or cut out for the child to choose from. You can tape the menus to the wall in a classroom or work area. You could attach them to a writing notebook or binder. Or you can even photocopy them small, then turn them into a reminder band or bracelet to wear!

They give suggested sequences for the strategies in each of the five different areas we've discussed in the book: big body stuff, helping your eyes out, when your hands feel tired, when it's hard to focus, and when all the body sensations just get too much.

In this section, you'll also find a blank template to use if a child wants to try out their own tailored mixture of the strategies in the book, to meet their specific needs—maybe with a mixture of strategies from all five areas.

Print out the sheets, and then cut out relevant strategies, exercises, and tools from whichever area/s you find to best fit to your child, then glue them into the blank template!

BIG BODY STUFF

| 1. Foot Stool | 2. Pencil Choice | 3. Wedge Cushion | 4. Gel-Filled Cushion |
| 5. Trace the 8 | 6. Wrist Cross Ankle Cross | 7. Feel My Body | 8. Write! |

HELPING YOUR EYES OUT

| 1. Fun Paper Choices | 2. I-Spy Bean Bags | 3. Mirror Me Moves | 4. Eye Break/Scans |
| 5. Pencil to Nose | 6. My Eye Muscle | 7. Reversals Workbook | 8. Write! |

WHEN YOUR HANDS JUST FEEL TIRED

1. Hand Stamina Exercises Reminder Bookmark

2. Slantboard/Pencil Grips/ Erasable Pens

3. Motor Tool Box

4. Handwriting Reminder Bookmarks

5. My Handwriting Workbook

6. Write!

WHEN IT'S HARD TO FOCUS

1. Soft 2B Pencils

2. Yoga Ball/Yoga Ball Chair

3. Metronome/Visual Timer

4. Noise-Reducing Headphones/Visual Blocking Folder

5. Toe Touch Cross

6. Write!

WHEN MY BODY FEELS TOO MUCH
(OR TOO LITTLE)

1. Sensory Bin Writing	**2.** Shoulder Press	**3.** Play Dough Writing	**4.** Head Below Knees
5. Velcro Dots/ Spiky Pencil Grip/ Weighted Pencil Grip	**6.** Mantra	**7.** Write!	

CREATE YOUR OWN WRITING STRATEGIES ROUTINE

_____ 's Writing Schedule			
1.	2.	3.	4.
5.	6.	7.	8. Write!

Big Body Stuff

Foot Stool		Trace the 8	
Pencil Choice		Wrist Cross Ankle Cross	
Wedge Cushion		Feel My Body	
Gel-Filled Cushion			

Helping Your Eyes Out

Fun Paper Choices		Eye Scans	
I-Spy Bean Bags		Pencil to Nose	
Mirror Me Moves		My Eye Muscle Workbook	
Eye Break		My Reversals Workbook	

When Your Hands Just Feel Tired

Hand Stamina Exercise Reminder Bookmark		Motor Tool Box	
Slantboard		Handwriting Reminder Bookmarks	
Pencil Grips		My Handwriting Workbook	
Erasable Pens			

When it's Hard to Focus

Soft 2B Pencils		Noise-Reducing Headphones	
Yoga Ball/Yoga Ball Chair		Visual Blocking Folder	
Metronome		Toe Touch Cross	
Visual Timer			

When All Your Body's Feelings and Senses Get Too Much (or Too Little)			
Sensory Bin Writing		Velcro Dots	
Shoulder Press		Spiky Pencil Grip	
Play Dough Writing		Weighted Pencil Grip	
Head Below Knees		Mantra	

Bookmarks

Cut out and laminate these Reminder Bookmarks. Or you can make your own based on what you've found works best for you, as you work through all the chapters.

Why don't you keep a copy on your desk or table, or in your Motor Tool Box?

HAND WARM-UP EXERCISE REMINDER BOOKMARKS

These bookmarks are a reminder of the Hand Warm-Up Exercise you can do as often as possible. They're great for writing stamina too!

Hand Warm-Up Exercise

1. Shake out both hands.

2. Open and close both hands 5–10 times.

3. Press palms together and hold for 10 seconds.

4. Seat push up: with flat palms and feet planted on the floor, push up from your chair and hold for 10 seconds.

Hand Warm-Up Exercise

1. Shake out both hands.

2. Open and close both hands 5–10 times.

3. Press palms together and hold for 10 seconds.

4. Seat push up: with flat palms and feet planted on the floor, push up from your chair and hold for 10 seconds.

KEEP TRACK OF MY WRITING

This bookmark helps you make sure you are keeping track of all of your handwriting goals and checking over your work as you write.

Before I begin writing...

1. I will write neatly.

2. I will write on the lines.

3. I will put spaces between my words.

4. My letters will be the same size.

5. I will use punctuation and capitalization.

6. I will spell the words I know the best that I can.

7. If I need a re-focuser, I can do so from my seat and get back to work.

8. If I am feeling like I really have to move, I can ask my teacher for a quick two-minute standing exercise break.

Before I begin writing...

1. I will write neatly.

2. I will write on the lines.
   Aa Bb

3. I will put spaces between my words.
   I can put spaces!

4. My letters will be the same size.
   Hello

5. I will use punctuation and capitalization.
    Do you want to get some pizza, David?

6. I will spell the words I know the best that I can.
   Sight words

7. If I need a re-focuser, I can do so from my seat and get back to work.

8. If I am feeling like I really have to move, I can ask my teacher for a quick two-minute standing exercise break.

MY WRITING GOALS

Directions for the child: It's your turn to be an editor of your own work. I know from seeing what my own editor does, it can be a big job! It's a really important role, though, because it helps your work look and sound great! The tips included on these bookmarks are helpful and quick reminders for you to use as you write. Especially when you have lots and lots of ideas in your head, it can be difficult to write neatly, with the correct capitalization, on the lines, with spacing, etc. Use the tips on these bookmarks around every paragraph to go over each sentence, and fix, or edit, your work, to make sure you followed each "rule" listed.

Grown-ups: This is for older kids who are self-monitoring their handwriting. Laminate these bookmarks to add to your writing center. Depending on the student, you can fill in the number of paragraphs you want them to write before coming back to the self-monitoring writing checklist. You can glue this to the other bookmark, and laminate them together—as a before and after self-monitoring writing checklist.

My Writing Goals...

1. Neatness.

2. Writing on the lines.

3. Spacing between words.

4. Letters being the same size.

5. Punctuation and capitalization.

6. Spelling of sight words the best that I can.

7. If I need a re-focuser, I can do so from my seat and get back to work.

8. If I am feeling like I really have to move, I can ask my teacher for a quick 2-minute standing exercise break.

My Writing Goals...

1.

2.

3.

4.

5.

6.

7.

8.

Laminates to Go in the Workbooks

EYE SCAN EXERCISE

You can place this exercise near where you keep your child's writing and/or reading tools and laminate it for increased durability. This will also encourage children to utilize the saccades exercise consistently as part of their daily routines.

Instructions:

1. Keep your head straight—only move your eyes!
2. Look at the smiley face.
3. Look at the check mark.
4. Repeat five times.

PAPER CHOICES

In Chapter 2 (Helping Your Eyes Out) we talked about fun paper choices. Here you can see whole page examples of each type of paper we spoke about. You can also download color versions of these fun paper types from.

It is important to note that as your child completes the activities in this book, and their handwriting progresses, the paper that works best for them may (and should!) change.

MY EYE MUSCLE WORKBOOK

Directions for the child: Complete a Helping Your Eyes Out worksheet from Chapter 2 once a day, as part of your writing schedule, if this is found to be your main area of difficulty impacting writing.

Grown-ups: Consider laminating these sheets so that your child can complete these sheets on a daily basis, using an erasable marker.

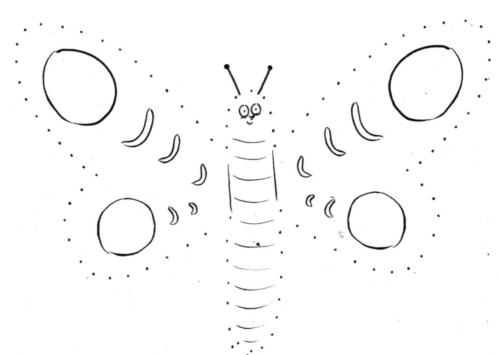

MY REVERSALS WORKBOOK

As with the eye muscle activities, these sheets can be laminated so the child can re-use them and practice daily. They can keep them in their reversals workbook.

Worksheets for the remaining letters in the alphabet are available to download from https://libraryjkp.papertrell.com/ redeem using the code VYOWUWA

Directions: Find and circle the b's.

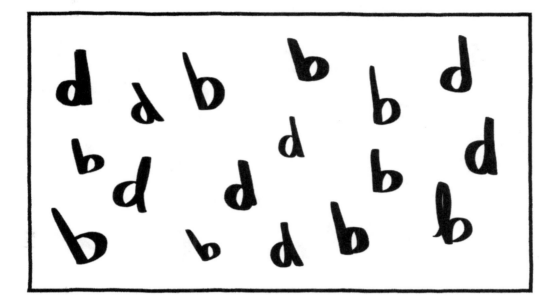

How many b's did you find?

Find the q's

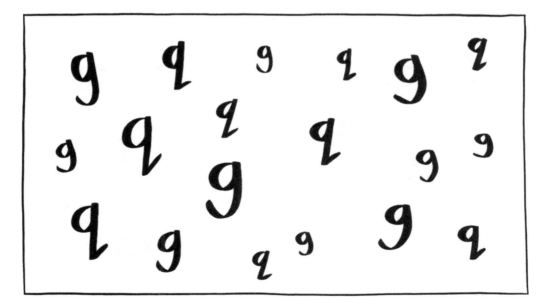

How many q's did you find?

Find the c's

a   c   C   a

d   a   c

a

C   C   C

a

c

C   a   a   a

C   a   c   C   a

How many c's did you find?

Find the a's

C   a   C   a   c   a

c   a   a   C   C

d   c   C   c

C   a   a   C   a   c

How many a's did you find?

Find the d's

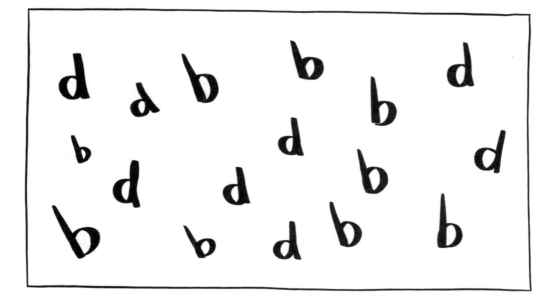

How many d's did you find?

Find the p's

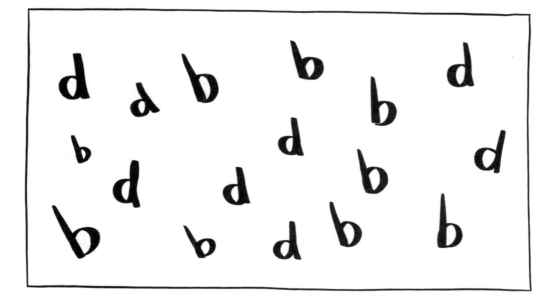

How many p's did you find?

Find the g's

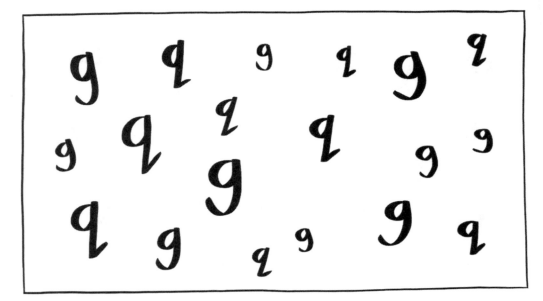

How many g's did you find?

Write out each commonly reversed letter five times

a ....

c ....

q ....

g ....

p ....

d ....

b ....

MY HANDWRITING WORKBOOK PAGES

Directions for the child: The following handwriting pages have letters and numbers in upper and lower case letters. They were designed to be laminated and used every day before you begin writing. Remember, the more you practice writing your letters, the easier it will be to put them into what we therapists call "muscle memory," where forming the letters correctly feels simple, as you have practiced it so often! Try and make this fun. Decorate your binder with stickers and markers—call it a silly name!

Grown-ups: Have your child/student do at least one page per day as part of their writing routine, if handwriting legibility, formation, and/or letter memory are areas of concern.

Upper Case Letter A (example)

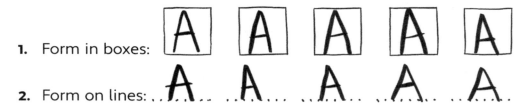

1. Form in boxes:

2. Form on lines:

3. Draw a picture in the box of something you like, or that makes you laugh and begins with the letter 'A'

Upper Case Letter A

1. Form in boxes: ☐ ☐ ☐ ☐ ☐

2. Form on lines: ....

3. Draw a picture in the box of something you like, or that makes you laugh and begins with the letter 'A'

☐

Lower Case Letter a

1. Form in boxes: ☐ ☐ ☐ ☐ ☐

2. Form on lines: ....

3. Draw a picture in the box of something you like, or that makes you laugh and begins with the letter 'a'

☐

Upper Case Letter B

1. Form in boxes:

2. Form on lines: . . . .

3. Draw a picture in the box of something you like, or that makes you laugh and begins with the letter 'B'

Lower Case Letter b

1. Form in boxes:

2. Form on lines: . . . .

3. Draw a picture in the box of something you like, or that makes you laugh and begins with the letter 'b'

Upper Case Letter C

1. Form in boxes:

2. Form on lines: ....

3. Draw a picture in the box of something you like, or that makes you laugh and begins with the letter 'C'

Lower Case Letter c

1. Form in boxes:

2. Form on lines: ....

3. Draw a picture in the box of something you like, or that makes you laugh and begins with the letter 'c'

Upper Case Letter D

1. Form in boxes:

2. Form on lines: . . , ...

3. Draw a picture in the box of something you like, or that makes you laugh and begins with the letter 'c'

Lower Case Letter d

1. Form in boxes:

2. Form on lines: . . . .

3. Draw a picture in the box of something you like, or that makes you laugh and begins with the letter 'd'

Upper Case Letter E

1. Form in boxes: ☐ ☐ ☐ ☐ ☐

2. Form on lines: ....

3. Draw a picture in the box of something you like, or that makes you laugh and begins with the letter 'e'

[blank box]

Lower Case Letter e

1. Form in boxes: ☐ ☐ ☐ ☐ ☐

2. Form on lines: ....

3. Draw a picture in the box of something you like, or that makes you laugh and begins with the letter 'e'

[blank box]

Upper Case Letter F

1. Form in boxes:

2. Form on lines: . . . .

3. Draw a picture in the box of something you like, or that makes you laugh and begins with the letter 'F'

Lower Case Letter f

1. Form in boxes:

2. Form on lines: . . . .

3. Draw a picture in the box of something you like, or that makes you laugh and begins with the letter 'f'

Glossary

Cognitive perception: The way that we process and actively make sense of the information that our senses receive from our environment (such as remembering, learning, and problem-solving).

Fine motor (also known as dexterity): The ability to make small movements using the small movements of the hands and fingers.

Gross motor: Large movements of the legs, arms, and torso.

Ocular motor: The eyes' ability to locate and fixate on an object in the field of vision. There are three types of movements, including fixations (the ability to hold the eyes steady without moving off the target), saccades (the ability of the eyes to accurately jump as they change targets), and pursuits (the ability of the eyes to follow a moving target).

Proprioception: Awareness of the position and movement of the body. Receptors are primarily located in the muscles.

Self-regulation: The ability to connect our body and mind and manage related feelings in reaction to challenging situations through the use of connected strategies.

Social and emotional learning: The ability to manage feelings and behaviors, understand the feelings of others, get along with others, and build relationships with others. Social and emotional learning skills assist in developing abilities in paying attention, self-control, cooperation, and following directions.

Vestibular: Sense of balance and spatial orientation. The receptor is located in the inner ear.

Visual motor: Visual motor skills are also called visual motor integration skills. They emerge from the integration of visual skills, visual perceptual skills, and motor skills. They demonstrate our ability to visually take in information and successfully draw or copy items or perform constructive activities in a motoric manner.

Visual perception: The brain's ability to make sense of and interpret what the eyes are seeing.

Recommended Reading

AOTA Practice Advisory on Occupational Therapy in Response to Intervention (2012). Available at: www. aota.org/-/media/corporate/files/practice/children/ browse/school/RtI/AOTA%20RtI%20practice%20Adv%20 final%20%20101612.pdf.

Attention Deficit Hyperactivity Disorder overview. National Institute of Mental Health. www.nimh.nih. gov/health/topics/attention-deficit-hyperactivity-disorder-adhd/index.shtml.

Bedell, G., Fertel-Daly, D. and Hinojosa, J. (2001) "Effects of a weighted vest on attention to task and self-stimulatory behaviors in preschools with pervasive developmental disorders." *American Journal of Occupational Therapy*, 55: 6.

Burns, M. (2010) "Response-to-intervention research: is the sum of the parts as great as the whole?" *Perspectives on Language and Literacy*, 36: 2. Available at: www.rtinetwork.org/learn/research/ response-to-intervention-research-is-the-sum-of-the-parts-as-great-as-the-whole.

Chuang, K-J., Chen, H-W., Liu, I-J. *et al.* (2012) "The effect of essential oil on heart rate and blood pressure among solus por aqua workers." *European Association of Preventive Cardiology*. Published online.

Jennings, D., Hanline, M.F. and Woods, J. (2012) "Using routines-based interventions in early childhood special education." *Dimensions of Early Childhood*, 40: 2. Available at: https://www.frontiersin.org/ articles/10.3389/fnint.2010.00008/full.

Laverdure, P., Cosbey, J., Gaylord, H. and LeCompte, B. (2017) *Providing Collaborative and Contextual Service in School Contexts and Environments*. American Occupational Therapy Association. Available at: www.aota.org/~/media/Corporate/Files/Publications/ CE-Articles/CE-Article-August-2017.pdf.

Miller, L., Neilsen, D.M. and Schoen, S. (2012) "Attention deficit hyperactivity disorder and sensory modulation disorder: A comparison of behavior and physiology." *Research in Developmental Disabilities*, 33: 808–818.

Quinn, P. and Gehret, J. (n.d.) *End the "I Can't Sleep" Cycle of Exhaustion*. Additude. Available at: www. additudemag.com/slideshow/22/slide-1.html.

Reynolds, S. and Lane, S. (2009) "Sensory overresponsivity and anxiety in children with ADHD." *American Journal of Occupational Therapy*, 63: 433–440.

Schaaf, R.C., Benevides, T., Blanche, E.I., *et al.* (2010) "Parasympathetic functions in children with sensory processing disorder." *Frontiers in Integrative Neuroscience*. Published online: doi 10.3389/ fnint.2010.00004.

OTHER TITLES BY LAUREN BRUKNER

Self-Control to the Rescue!
Super Powers to Help Kids Through the
Tough Stuff in Everyday Life
Lauren Brukner
Illustrated by Apsley
ISBN 978 1 78592 759 1
eISBN 978 1 78450 619 3

———

Stay Cool and In Control with the Keep-Calm Guru
Wise Ways for Children to Regulate
their Emotions and Senses
Lauren Brukner
Illustrated by Apsley
ISBN 978 1 78592 714 0
eISBN 978 1 78450 300 0

———

How to Be a Superhero Called Self-Control!
Super Powers to Help Younger Children to
Regulate their Emotions and Senses
Lauren Brukner
Illustrated by Apsley
ISBN 978 1 84905 717 2
eISBN 978 1 78450 203 4

———

The Kids' Guide to Staying Awesome and In Control
Simple Stuff to Help Children Regulate
their Emotions and Senses
Lauren Brukner
ISBN 978 1 84905 997 8
eISBN 978 0 85700 962 3

———